MIDGES IN SCOTLAND

MIDGES IN SCOTLAND

George Hendry

Cartoons by *BAX*

ABERDEEN UNIVERSITY PRESS

First published 1989
Aberdeen University Press
A member of the Pergamon Group

© George Hendry 1989

British Library Cataloguing in Publication Data

Hendry, George
  Midges in Scotland.
  1. Great Britain. Flies
  I. Title
  595.77′0941

  ISBN 0 08 036595 7

PRINTED IN GREAT BRITAIN
THE UNIVERSITY PRESS
ABERDEEN

CONTENTS

ACKNOWLEDGEMENTS

The author acknowledges with gratitude the advice, assistance and information from Professor Douglas Kettle, John Boorman, Mike Birley and Eric Reye on many midgy matters.

PREAMBLE

For years there has been a wee conspiracy that the midges should never be discussed in front of the tourists. By mentioning not a word about midges in the holiday-guides to Scotland, let alone giving simple advice on living with midges, in some way it is hoped that the midge problem will go away. Unfortunately the midges will not go away and, year after year, the visitors are driven to distraction and even to dislike the Scottish Highlands. Fortunately many people do learn to live with the midges and to enjoy Scotland in all its seasons.

This account sets out to describe in fairly brief terms how, when and why midges bite, to say something about their biology and to consider ways of avoiding the worst assaults of a midge pack in full cry. Over the years many attempts have been made to control midges, both in Scotland and overseas, sometimes with considerable success, more often resulting in a costly failure. Generally the midge has the last word in these conflicts with Man. At the very least then, this book will give the visitor and Highlander the satisfaction of knowing their common enemy. By understanding the ways of the midge, a lot more people should be able to enjoy the full splendour of the Highland summer without quite so many bites!

INTRODUCTION

The proximity of the biting midge and the wearing of
the kilt gave rise to the Highland fling! This is
probably the only joke that can be made about an
insect which has long been a curse of the Highland
summers. Like their relatives, the mosquitoes, it is
the female midges which bite to secure a blood-meal
for their developing eggs. Despite plagues of biting
midges in the Canadian outback, in Siberia, on the
sun-drenched beaches of Australia and the
Caribbean, eminent travellers and experienced
zoologists alike agree that some of the fiercest midges
in the world are to be found in the Highlands of
Scotland. Wherever they abound, midges cause
discomfort, misery and some pain to warm-blooded
animals and humans. Social barriers they ignore.
Attacks are made on the high and low with
indifference. It was biting midges who half-
devoured Queen Victoria at a Sutherland picnic
according to her diary of 1872. Turning their
attention to lesser mortals, midges were held
responsible for serious delays in the building of the

Krasnoyarsk dam in Siberia in 1960. Few insects have achieved front-page coverage in *Pravda* under the headline 'This evil can be conquered'! Back in Scotland, forty years ago both the Scottish Tourist Board and the Secretary of State for Scotland, Tom Johnston, sponsored scientific research into ways of combating midges. Much of that research taught us a great deal about the peculiar ways of the Scottish midge. The research also showed that there are several profound and costly solutions to the problem and just a few rather simpler answers. These simple answers rely on an understanding of the unusual life-style of the biting midge.

Man has dwelt in the Highlands for the last 8000 years or so and in that time has learnt how to live with all sorts of insect life and for most of that time without the aid of sophisticated chemical sprays and insect repellents. It is still possible to enjoy the Highlands without the support of these toxins and many people do. There can be few more extra-ordinary sights in the Highlands than to see travellers on the platform of Achnasheen Station waiting for the arrival of the 8.20 train on a warm summer's evening. Word has it that the local midges only get up for feeding 15 minutes before the train arrives. In that short interval they get to work to savage the tired, hot, defenceless traveller. But what of the friendly station-master? He knows his midges too well and does just what his forefathers have done for generations. Come 8.20 p.m. and the train draws away for Inverness, the Highlands each summer night are given over to the midges. These creatures form a dominant and successful part of Scottish wildlife and by controlling man's activities in the Highlands they are the guardians of some of the most beautiful and unspoilt areas of Northern Europe. The Highlands would not be the same without the midges.

HISTORICAL PERSPECTIVE

The very word 'midge' is one originating deep in European pre-history, from the old Norse *muggia*, to the *mygg* of the Swedes, the *myg* of the Dutch and *mycg* of the Saxons. But despite its antiquity, the midge gets few references in the early literature of Scotland. Not one word is given by Tacitus in his account of his father-in-law Agricola's excursions into the Grampians around AD 80. One thing is certain, those bare thighs of the Roman Legions would have been sorely bitten as they struggled through the wetlands of Strathmore on their way north. Nor did the English host at Bannockburn pause in their flight to describe what it was like to have midges nibbling away under chain-mail or surcoat on that warm July day in 1314. One of the earliest references to Scottish midges comes from a fourteenth century tale of three travelling monks from Peebles who resorted to swatting midges with bundles of birch twigs.

Boswell in his 1773 tour of the Hebrides with Samuel Johnston, fancied himself being bitten by innumerable vermin. Robert Louis Stevenson in *Kidnapped* has his hero David Balfour sore troubled by the midges while hiding from the Redcoats.

It wasn't until 1713 that an Essex minister, the Rev William Derham set down one of the first scientific descriptions of the midge or nidiot as he called it. He knew it as a greedy blood-sucker 'endued with a spear'. Serious studies of the midge really began in the late nineteenth century in Britain, Belgium, Germany and Russia. By the 1930s much of the British midge fauna had been named and described in some detail in Edwards' block-buster of a book 'British Blood-sucking Flies' and later in greater detail in Campbell and Pelham-Clinton's classic account. (The second author was later honoured by the naming of a Scottish species first recognised in 1984 as *Culicoides clintoni*). In the years after the Second World War several more species were discovered lurking in the hills in Scotland including *C. scoticus, C. achrayi* (after Loch Achray in the Trossachs) and *C. duddingstoni* (after Duddingston Loch in Edinburgh). Today some thirty-four species of biting midge are known from Scotland. However as early as 1946 it was recognised that most of the attacks on humans were being carried out by just four or five species, of which one in particular was responsible for most of the trouble. This species enjoys the full scientific name of *Culicoides impunctatus* Goetghebuer, or more simply the Highland Midge.

In 1952 the University of Edinburgh set up a Midge Control Unit specifically to study ways of combating the Highland Midge. Under the direction of Dr (later Professor) Douglas Kettle a great deal was learnt about the life of the midge in Scotland and this work today forms the basis for our understanding of the creature. Combined with the efforts of scientists in the United States, Africa, Australia and Russia much is now known about midges, about their life-history, the way they reproduce, how they seek their victims, in short what makes them such vicious little biters. The story that has emerged is a fascinating example of dedicated study frequently conducted under difficult and often painful conditions out on the hills and moors. Today little active research is funded in Scotland but overseas new technologies are being explored to combat the species. One simple message has emerged from all this research. Almost all of the advances made in tackling the midge problem owe their successes to basic field and laboratory research into the life-history, the population dynamics, the genetics and the ecology of the insect. Without a sound understanding of how and why midges behave the way they do, then all the chemical sprayings, repellents and biological controls in the world become a waste of time, effort and money. The pity is that this simple message has not always been appreciated. Tourist boards, governments, local authorities, hoteliers and the tourists themselves want action now. The trigger finger on the chemical spray-gun gets very twitchy. It is only when expensive eradication campaigns fail, often spectacularly, that the call for more research is heeded.

Modern man's almost instinctive urge to reach for his spray-gun has proved, time after time, to be a costly mistake. Midges are insects and like all other insects as well as higher animals such as fish, birds or mammals, all can be poisoned if enough toxins are thrown at them. Any chemical used against midges, will, directly or indirectly, affect other harmless or even beneficial forms of life. It took twenty years to recognise this. Rachel Carson's book *Silent Spring*, which exposed the catastrophic effects on wildlife of the unregulated use of pesticides, had a profound effect on governments and scientists alike in the 1960s and today we have learnt to temper or suppress our urge to spray. The reward for striving for alternatives to spraying, particularly in North America and in Africa in the war against the mosquito and the tse-tse fly, has meant that today there are much more effective ways of tackling insect pests, ways which are less costly in terms of money and impact on the environment. To appreciate how these modern approaches work it is necessary to understand something of the world of the midge. The accounts which follow can only be a summary. For those whose appetite is unsatisfied, the short bibliography at the end will produce an open door to a fascinating world.

DISTRIBUTION

Biting midges are found world-wide and have exploited their peculiar talents over much of the land surface of the globe. Most exploit the advantage of diminutive size. Many species prey on other insects. Others have evolved to feed undetected on a wide range of warm-blooded mammals or birds. Just a few have acquired a taste for human blood. Some 900 species of the most important genus *Culicoides* have been described so far, principally from sub-arctic and temperate Europe, Asia, north and central America, Australia and out to the smaller islands of the Pacific. Related genera are known from the tropical Caribbean seashores to the heights of Everest where the 1921 expedition complained of being persistently bitten at 14,000 feet. In Scotland, most of the thirty-four known species confine their blood-sucking practices to cattle, sheep, horses and deer. A few prey on domestic fowl and birds, about four or occasionally five species attack humans. Most of the Scottish species have a distinct, often local distribution. Some restrict themselves to farm-yards and dung-heaps, others to sea or loch shores, a few to salt-marshes, mires or woodlands. Of the most persistent man-biters, just one species *Culicoides impunctatus* dominates in upland Britain where it accounts for more than 90 per cent of the recorded attacks. There is some indication that the *C. impunctatus* population in Scotland may be a race distinct from the *C. impunctatus* midges found over the border in England and in continental Europe. If this can be proven it would go some way to explain why the midges of Scotland have such a vicious reputation. The Scots who live in towns or in the Lowlands have learnt to live with another species *C. obsoletus* or the Garden Midge. There is nothing obsolete about the way this midge bites; it does so less painfully than its Highland cousin but it is infuriatingly persistent. This species can be found throughout Europe, Asia, into Canada and the United States. A rather more painful biter, fairly common on the Scottish coastal salt-marshes, is likely to be *C. halophilus*, while down on the farm another species *C. nubeculosus* will attack humans, particularly in stables and byres and around closely packed cattle. There are several other midge species which will have a go at humans from time to time but they are rarely much trouble. It remains true, however, that no natural habitat or location in Scotland can be considered to be entirely midge free. Biting episodes in the hills above 1,500 feet may be reduced but in sheltered corries midges can be active at considerable elevations. Nor is water a barrier. No less than three species of midge have been recorded from St Kilda lying out in the Atlantic nearly 100 miles from the Scottish mainland. Only in densely developed cities and towns, are midges generally considered to be a trivial nuisance, though even there the Garden Midge can get a hold on town parks and golf courses in wet summers. The banks of the River Kelvin, half a mile from the centre of Glasgow, are a well known midge-infested haunt in high summer.

WHAT IS A MIDGE?

As members of the Diptera (the two-winged flies), biting midges share several features in common with their relatives the mosquitoes, sandflies and blackflies. Biting midges, however, are particularly small with a wingspan of usually less than 2 mm. The Highland Midge is diminutive with a wingspan of only about 1.4 mm, a feature emphasised by its Gaelic name *Meanbh chuileag* (tiny fly). Any doubts about recognising a biting midge can be quickly settled by looking for the characteristic blotches or dark-flecked spots on the membranous wings. These spots can be readily seen using a low-powered hand-lens and are important, at least to taxonomists, in identifying one midge species from another. For example, the distinctive pattern of six to seven separate blotches on the wing of the Highland Midge is quite different from the arrangement of spots on the wing of the Garden Midge. If these dark patches cannot be seen on a living specimen then it is unlikely to be a biting midge. Once seen there is no mistaking it.

Another unusual characteristic of biting midges is the way they fold their wings scissor-like when at rest or when biting and feeding. The generally larger and more colourful mosquitoes and related flies usually hold their wings roof-like when at rest. The most likely insect to be confused with the biting midge is the Chironomid or dancing midge. These

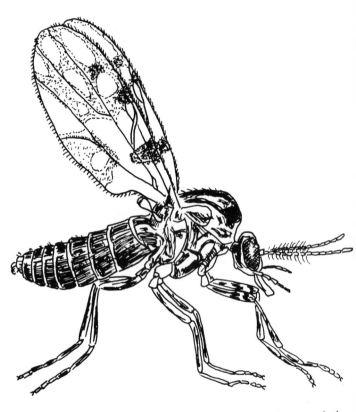

The Highland Midge in flight. Note the characteristic markings on the single pair of wings.

The Highland Midge at rest, or while feeding, with wings
crossed scissor-like over the abdomen.

insects, common in spring, summer and often well into late autumn, are significantly larger than biting midges, they don't bite and are most frequently observed as obvious, often dense, dancing swarms. There the insects, usually males, hover and fly backwards and forwards for short distances but always facing the same direction usually head into the wind. They will often occupy a favoured site for weeks at a time. If these dancing midges are displaced accidentally or deliberately they neither bite nor sting. Their sole interest in forming these dancing swarms is to attract females for reproduction. Instead they frequently get swatted in mistake for the real culprit, the smaller biting midge. Gatherings of biting midges do occur but they are much less populous and rarely obvious except to the trained eye.

Like other blood-sucking insects, the female midge has a well-developed, specialised, mouth enabling her both to pierce the skin of her victim as well as to suck up the released blood. Piercing the skin is done by a pair of finely-toothed elongated mandibles and maxillae which work backwards and forwards with a scissor-like action, cutting ever deeper into the skin surface. When the cut or wound is deep enough a pool of blood is released from the fine capillary vessels underlying the skin. At this point the midge quickly shapes or rolls its mouth-parts into a fine tube or food-canal which is inserted into the wound to draw up the free-flowing blood. In mosquitoes and, in all probability, in midges too, saliva is pumped into the wound to prevent the blood from clotting and the flow from drying up. This saliva with its digestive enzymes now induces in the victims a mild allergic or immune response causing the victim, human or otherwise, to counter-respond with a rush of histamine to the site of the wound. One of the immediate effects of the histamine is to cause the wounded capillary vessel to open up for a few minutes to enable the body to mobilise and send in certain white blood-cells which in turn set about the task of eliminating any infection and repairing the wound. Those few minutes between breaking into the blood-vessel and the body repairing the wound and staunching the blood-flow are a vital period to the midge. If left undisturbed, the midge will feed for up to 3 or 4 minutes before disengaging. Much of the itching and swelling of the wound area follows from the activities of the healthy body's natural repair machinery. The female midge has evolved its feeding habits to exploit the small time-lag before the blood-vessel closes down. A ticklish task for one so small. The male midge on the other hand has a simpler, less specialised, mouth; it doesn't bite animals and for that reason has been less studied scientifically. It is believed that the males derive all their food-requirements from plant nectar and from rotting plant remains. They are then of no direct trouble to humans.

BITES AND THE BITING HABIT

One bite from a midge is insignificant, for most people passing unnoticed. However midges rarely work in ones. The evening stimulus for feeding affects large populations of pregnant and hungry females and it is this concerted and simultaneous assault, involving perhaps dozens of midges, often concentrated over 20 or 30 minutes which drives grown men to distraction and to seek shelter or relief from the maddening pursuits of an obsessive but unseen tormentor. Despite this, a number of dedicated scientists have sat it out and methodically recorded midge bites at the rate of 2,000 to 3,000 bites an hour. By this means a fair amount is known about midge behaviour. Having first detected its victim mainly by body odours (which may include the very carbon dioxide exhaled in breathing) the midge homes in and attempts to land unnoticed on exposed skin. The close approach is probably conducted using the insect's eyesight rather than its sense of smell. If the landing is successful the midge will often wander over the surface of the skin presumably searching for a suitable soft area before beginning the task of cutting into the epidermis. Sometimes several false or abandoned attempts will be made before a satisfactory wound is secured. So far the victim will have felt little or no pain. If the midge continues to escape unwelcome attention, some 3 to 4 minutes will be spent feeding on blood.

It is early in this period that the victim becomes first aware of a slight but persistent stinging or pricking sensation. If the midge can secure its meal without interruption it will finally disengage its mouth-parts and retire, fully gorged, for a rest period. If, as may often happen, feeding is interrupted, then the midge will show its remarkable powers of single-minded obsessive persistence when it will return again and again until it has secured its full quota of blood. Less than 0.1 μl (one ten-millionth of a litre) of blood is taken, an insignificantly small amount for the average human adult with about 5.6 litres to spare. To most people the overall result is no more than a mildly irritating spot, which subsides within a few minutes. But in the smaller number of susceptible victims the spots may rise to resemble nettle-rash accompanied by a puffiness of the affected area particularly over the forehead, eyelid and lips. How each person responds depends, in part, on how often he or she has been exposed to midge bites before. To first-time visitors to the Highlands, the response to being bitten is minimal; this happy state lasting perhaps for three to four days. These lucky souls have an immune system which has not been triggered to respond to midge bites, or more probably to certain proteins in the midge saliva. Because they have no anti-midge antibodies with which to recognise midge saliva, the bite has no noticeable effect. But, unfortunately, this state of innocence has to end; with increasing exposure to attacks, the body's immune system reacts. In the blood-stream antibodies are released which specifically respond to the foreign proteins in midge saliva. So, on the next occasion when the midges attack, there is a rapid mobilisation of the defence and repair mechanisms that exist in every healthy person, leading to the inactivation of the midge saliva contents and repairs to the wound. The natural and healthy response of the immune system is to pump histamine into the site of the fresh wound to prepare the way for the protective work to be done by the white blood-cells. The result is a wound which is rapidly repaired and where the midge saliva is promptly detoxified. The price to be paid for all this healthy self-protection is that the victim is left with a mildly uncomfortable to slightly irritating spot, the irritation lasting for some few minutes. Most people, visitors and locals alike, respond in this way, given reasonably good health. A very few people over-respond by becoming quite ill and have to seek prompt medical attention. Their immune responses are rather too active. However, these unfortunate souls are usually well aware of their condition, often because they know that their bodies over-react to bites or stings from other kinds of insects. Among the local population, including long-term settlers, some individuals, but by no means all, develop a much more controlled, slow and less severe reaction to midge bites. These are the fortunate, seemingly enviable crofters who appear to escape the attention of the midges. They don't. It is only that with years of exposure to midge bites their immune system is rather slow to respond. Bee-keepers with years of experience similarly show a sluggish response when they are stung by bees. If it is any consolation there are a great many Highlanders who to their dying day suffer just as much as the tourist after the first week of a holiday in the area. The difference, however, is that these Highlanders have a knack of predicting when and where the midges are going to be out. Forewarned they know what to do to avoid the worst of the attacks.

WHEN AND WHY DO MIDGES BITE?

Seasonally, in Scotland, several midge species are active from April until October. These early and late-season fliers are rarely of much trouble to humans. The Highland Midge, *C. impunctatus*, first appears on the wing towards the end of May or in early June. Most of this early hatch are non-biting males who have no interest in molesting humans. The first serious biting episodes really begin in mid-June and persist to varying degrees of severity throughout July and into August. The biting season lasts for about 12 weeks. Towards the end of August midge numbers decline rapidly, just as many tourists turn south. By mid-September the midges are no longer an intolerable problem. The attacks are less prolonged and rarely more than a slight nuisance, although in some years, given a mild wet late summer there may be one or two last-ditch assaults until the end of the month. The Garden Midge, *C. obsoletus*, lingers on into October in sheltered or coastal areas. Its bite is much less irritating and may even pass unnoticed. For most people, from September until the following June, the midges can be quietly forgotten, allowing the Highlands to be enjoyed to their full. Seasoned visitors to Scotland know that the Highlands are often at their best outside the midge season; the visitors can enjoy their hard-earned holiday without fear of a bite. For those who prefer to visit during the summer months there is still much that can be done to avoid at least the worst effects of the attacks.

Few midges, in Britain, are active biters throughout the daylight hours. The aptly-named *C. heliophilus* (sun-lover) is an exception and prefers to bite around high noon. It is, however, much less common than the Highland Midge. Like most of the Scottish species, the Highland Midge is particularly sensitive to light and, subject to weather conditions, bites most vigorously towards the long evening twilight. The first stimulus for biting in this species occurs towards sunset as the radiation from the sun declines to below 260 W/m². (In Scotland full sunlight on a cloudless noon in mid-summer is about 800 W/m²). As the radiation decreases and the light fades, so midge activity begins. And as the sun radiation declines further to about 130 W/m², as happens at sunset on a cloudless midsummer evening, this is the moment for clouds of midges to rise from the ground cover and from tree trunks on which they have been sheltering. What often puzzles people is why midges so often bite earlier in the day. The explanation is that high unbroken cloud, even at mid-day, can reduce the radiation from the sun to below the critical 260 W/m². Thick low white clouds will take the radiation down to even lower levels as will dark rain-clouds. It is this cloudy weather which brings the midges out to bite in the morning or afternoon. In the forests, even on a cloudless day, the deep shade stimulates midges to bite for much of the daylight hours.

The apparent association of midges with warm humid weather is more to do with the cloud cover and lack of wind than humidity itself. Midges will bite avidly on dry evenings as the sun goes down. Humidity from a dry 65 per cent up to a moist 100 per cent has little effect on the intensity of biting though there is some indication that midges fly higher when the humidity is high and descend closer to the ground in dry weather. But whether they bite on the ankles or face, both can be mighty irritating. Drizzling rain does not deter activity either. Indeed midges and drizzle often go together on the West Coast if only because where there is drizzle there is cloud and cloud means reduced light intensity.

The Highland Midge is pretty hardy; it appears to be indifferent to all but unseasonally low temperatures, intense biting activities being maintained over the range 6° to 18° C. However, wind does severely limit midge assaults. At speeds of 2.5 m./second (about 5.5. mph), that is up to a slight breeze, midge biting continues unabated. But above this

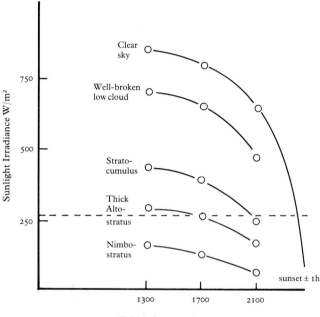

Sunlight irradiance through various types of cloud in mid-Scotland (latitude 60° N) at midsummer, in the course of the afternoon and evening. With increasingly thick and lower clouds sunlight penetration is reduced and irradiance falls to below 260 W/m², the trigger for midge activity.

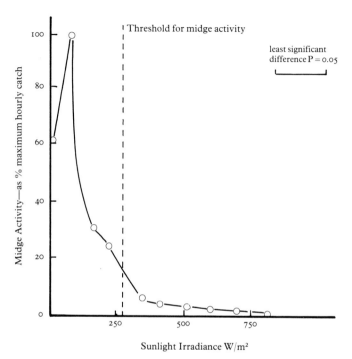

Sunlight Irradiance W/m²

Flying activity of the Highland Midge in relation to sunlight irradiance. As irradiance increases above 260 W/m², so midge activity is suppressed. When sunlight falls to about 100 to 130 W/m², midge activity reaches its maximum.

wind-speed they are forced to seek shelter usually on ground vegetation or, where available, on dark coloured tree-trunks. Young conifer plantations and thick unburnt heather appear to offer suitable sanctuary from the wind. But once the wind passes and calm airs prevail, clouds of midges can be seen rising in unison, anxious to get on with the task of securing a meal.

Taking all environmental components into account, the most important single factor which determines the intensity of the biting activity is light. Cloudless days and the midges will not stir until sunset. Dark rain-clouds and the midges are out in the middle of the day. In good summers, however, it is the prolonged evening and dawn twilight around mid-summer which offer an ideal environment for the Highland Midge. From mid-May until the end of July, twilight, at least the nautical definition of twilight, lasts throughout the night in mid-Scotland (latitude 56°N). It is no surprise, at least to campers, to find that midges can and frequently do continue biting into the small hours and again before dawn.

OTHER BITING INSECTS

Not every insect that bites of a summer evening is a midge. In Scotland there are other groups of flying blood-suckers, the Mosquito, Stable fly, Black fly and the notorious Cleg or Horse fly. All are much larger than midges. In addition there is a motley collection of rather more personalised biters, the Fleas, Lice and Bed bugs, rarely seen perhaps, but all too obvious when active. There are other biting insects in Scotland but for most people they are not common. The account which follows is then a very brief summary of the most common Scottish biters likely to be met in midge country and whose bite could be mistaken for that of a midge.

It surprises many people to learn that mosquitoes are to be found in Scotland, though perhaps not in the numbers of their smaller cousins. Of the thirty or so species of mosquito in the British Isles, all are several times larger than a midge. These two-winged, delicate long-legged insects have a wing-span of about 4 to 5 mm (say 1/4 inch), often with colourful iridescent or at least bi-coloured bodies. Like the midge, only the female hunts for blood before developing her eggs. Unlike midges, however, most mosquitoes lay their eggs on or close to water, though this need for water can be met by puddles, rain-water butts or gutters on houses. In Scotland there are four types of mosquitoes, those that persistently inhabit buildings, those breeding in woodlands, those found on the sea-shore or on coastal marshes and, fourthly, those of the field and moorland. Predictably almost all of those mosquitoes that share Man's dwellings or outbuildings will readily bite humans and domestic animals. Often known as house-gnats, many of these mosquitoes bite from April through to October. Those species which hibernate over winter may give the odd mid-winter nip if disturbed. One member of this group of household mosquitoes was responsible for the malaria, or ague as it was known, that persisted in the fenlands of east England up to the 1850s. Malaria today, in Britain, is extremely rare. Despite their harmlessness, the females continue to inflict a painful bite, mostly at night and often when the victim is asleep. These house mosquitoes are readily recognised by their high-pitched piping or singing, particularly when flying close to the ear.

The forest-dwelling mosquitoes are perhaps less often met with; they tend to bite only near their breeding sites. The coastal species, sometimes found on shore-line seaweed, can be vicious and persistent biters. Perhaps the most common mosquito outwith buildings and away from the seashore is one with the name *Aedes punctor*, characteristic of moorlands, heath, birch and pine forests. This common Scottish species lays its eggs in dry holes or depressions that fill up with water in winter. The adult female is particularly persistent in her attacks when a suitable blood-meal moves into her breeding grounds. Fortunately mosquitoes in this country probably no longer transmit diseases; they are merely irritating. And on the west coast, mosquitoes are, at worst, a minor nuisance.

A quite different biter is the Black Fly. This short-legged plump black insect with a wing-span of about 5 mm is a scourge of Man in parts of northern Canada and Siberia. In several parts of Africa and India these flies carry tropical diseases. In the

British Isles one of the twenty native species is all
too familiar for its unpleasant habit of feeding on the
inside of horses' ears. At times they can cause
considerable distress in stables. A related species of
Black Fly is fairly common in the Scottish Lowlands
and on the east coast where it will attack Man with a
persistence which can be infuriating in the extreme.
Once again, as with midges and mosquitoes, it is the
female which does all the biting. The size of the
insect, so much larger than a midge, makes its
attention all too obvious.

For stealth, the Cleg or Horse Fly takes the prize.
The stoutly-built sombre dusky-grey female, often
working singly, alights so gently on its victim, horse,
cow or human, to make a small painless incision in
the flesh before slipping its mouth parts into the
wound. It will even bite through clothing or hair.
Left undisturbed, with its head down and tail cocked
up, it will feed for one or two minutes. It has the
audacity to make a second wound nearby if the first
proves unsatisfactory. The pain comes when feeding
is over, and the bite shows as a feint red ring which
can persist and remain irritable for several days.
There is often a distinct swelling around the bitten
area. Clegs, unlike midges and many mosquitoes,
feed mainly during warm bright days and, in
Scotland at least, are less active in cool cloudy
weather. In the Highlands they are only common in
July and August. Clegs, mosquitoes and midges do
share one feature in common; their attraction to
dark-coloured clothing particularly when the wearer
is perspiring profusely.

Scotland also has biters related to the African Tse-Tse fly. Known here as the Stable Fly, it is similar in appearance to the common House Fly. Both males and females will attack horses, cattle and on occasions Man. At times their numbers can reach intolerable proportions. The eggs are laid on decaying plant matter, particularly wet soiled animal fodder which has been allowed to accumulate in byres and stables. Persistent outbreaks of large populations of Stable Flies are often a sign of poor animal hygiene.

Bed bugs, certain lice and fleas have long enjoyed Man's company. In these days of improved personal hygiene these parasites are less common than in previous centuries. However in times of natural disasters, such as earthquakes or hurricanes, where access to washing facilities or a change of clothing becomes difficult, so these creatures multiply bringing with them outbreaks of typhus and, in times past, bubonic plague. Today, for most people, their presence is harmless and at best an overnight irritant.

A more obvious irritant, particularly to bare-legged walkers and climbers, is the tick family. More closely related to spiders than insects, these round-bodied black or brown parasites rest on tall grasses waiting for a bare leg to brush past. Having transferred itself to its new-found host, the tick sinks its head painlessly into the victim's flesh where it will hang for hours, its soft body swelling to a considerable size before dropping off fully gorged. Ticks should not be pulled out. This will merely leave behind the pincers or proboscis and so introduce infection. Instead a lighted cigarette or heated matchstick, even a dose of whisky (applied to the tick) will usually encourage it to release its hold. A sterilised needle may be needed to prise out any remains. While Man has his share of annoyance from biting flies, his farm animals, deer, rabbits and birds appear to have more than their share. Apart from Horse and Stable Flies, many large animals suffer the almost constant attention of Ticks, Keds, Warble Flies, several species of Black flies as well as mosquitoes and, invariably in Scotland, several kinds of midge. Although veterinary science has helped to reduce the scourge of warble and ticks in cattle, wild deer continue to suffer fierce attacks. Rabbits have their fleas, the vector for the myxamatosis virus.

There is some good news among this unpleasant story, at least for humans. For most people, away from byres, poultry sheds or horse stables, many of these biting insects are not common. Most are readily dissuaded from attacking humans by the application of repellents marketed as midge repellents. For most people, by far the most frequent biter in Scotland, particularly in the west and north, is the midge. With the possible exception of the Highland Midge, the Cleg and perhaps one or two species of mosquito, most flying blood-sucking insects show a marked preference for cattle, sheep, deer or birds. Only when disturbed from their natural or preferred host will they take to humans. So most summer visitors to the Highlands will rarely experience the attention of Stable Flies or Black Flies, although almost certainly a mosquito or two will make an evening attack. Visitors from the south, however, will experience far more bites from mosquitoes back at home. The average English cottage garden has quite a collection of mosquitoes and no holiday in Italy is complete without a fair number of mosquito bites. American visitors may be relieved to see the back of their mosquito population, though they may not be too enamoured with the Scottish midge. Clegs are occasionally a real nuisance for perhaps two months of high summer in Scotland, but in Germany and parts of France they are active biters from April to the end of October.

To put all this into context, many biting insects that are common in Europe, in England and North America have their counterpart in Scotland but in most cases in relatively low numbers. The ecology of the landscape, the climate and particularly the high rainfall have tilted the balance in favour of just one group of biters, the midges. The rest of the biting insects seem to be, at times, almost a welcome conversational diversion.

BITING AND DISEASE

Many important diseases are harboured and transmitted by biting insects, particularly in the tropics. These include malaria and yellow fever by several species of mosquitoes, sleeping sickness by tse-tse flies and river blindness by blackflies. Concern about the role of midges as carriers of disease is natural and this possibility has been studied by scientists, medical entomologists and veterinary surgeons for many years.

The majority of biting midge species, including those in Scotland, feed on more than one host. The most commonly recorded victims are man, his domesticated animals, many wild animals including deer, rabbits and wild birds. It seems that both the Highland and the Garden Midge prefer to attack Man but this may simply reflect the presence of human observers. Both of these species of midge are a plague on cattle, horses, sheep, deer and even poultry. Despite their wide tastes, in terms of disease transmission to humans the Scottish midges are, as far as we know, harmless. Several species do, however cause extreme misery to horses, sheep and cattle. Deer herds both in Scotland and in Russia have been recorded as being driven out of low-lying pastures by midges and forced to seek relief on the impoverished slopes of the high hills. Midges may be one of the reasons why, until recent years, the Scottish Red Deer was an ill-fed and poorly developed specimen compared with its European cousins. Midges have long been blamed for distress in cows and in bad midgy summers may be responsible for declines in milk-yields. Several unpleasant disorders of horses, sweet itch, fistulous withers or poll evil are now known to be caused by various species of midge. Some of these species show a marked preference for biting particular areas of the mane, belly or flank and to persist in attacking the same area. Fortunately treatments are possible both to prevent and to cure these disorders. Much more serious, however, are the midge-borne diseases found overseas particularly in the sub-tropics and tropics. There, several midge species transmit a number of serious viral and protozoan diseases to sheep, cattle and horses as well as to the indigenous wild animals. In recent years a number of outbreaks of these diseases have resulted in considerable economic losses to the farming communities in these countries and have provoked active veterinary research in the United States, parts of Africa, central America and in Australia. Outbreaks of one important disease in sheep and cattle, Blue Tongue Virus, have been notified in a number of Mediterranean countries in recent years. So far, there are no confirmed reports of these diseases in Northern Europe. (However it is worth noting that our otherwise fairly innocuous Garden Midge (*C. obsoletus*) is closely related to one of those transmitting Blue Tongue in the United States.

Humans appear to be more fortunate. Apart from a few relatively minor disorders in the Caribbean and Central America there is no hard evidence that midges transmit diseases to human beings. Over the years midges have time and again been suspected of being a hazard to human health but have usually emerged with a clean ticket. In recent times there has been speculation that the AIDS viruses (HIV) might be transmitted by biting insects. Several authorities have examined this possibility but the consensus is that the AIDS viruses, almost certainly, are not transmitted by mosquitoes, close cousins of the biting midge. One simple observation is that AIDS itself or the antibodies to the virus are found only in sexually active adults and, with a few well-explained exceptions, are not found in children nor in the very elderly. Yet mosquitoes (and midges) bite the young, middle-aged and old without dis-crimination. Likewise mosquitoes and midges bite both sexes avidly. Indeed there is some evidence that certain midge species are attracted more to women than to men. The essence of these observations is that the pattern of the spread and development of the AIDS disease in human communities bears no resemblance to the biting behaviour and preferences of midges. This is particularly true in Europe where the disease is confined very largely to the male adult population. In addition to this powerful evidence, scientists have been unable to prove that the virus can even survive within an insect let alone be transmitted by one. Were it otherwise, the consequences are too horrific to contemplate.

LIFE CYCLE—THE KEY TO SUCCESS

One of the reasons for the success of midges in Scotland is their unusual life-pattern, one which has evolved to become well adapted to the Scottish environment. Like most insects, the midge undergoes several distinct stages of development, from egg to larva, to pupa before emerging as the familiar flying adult. However, with midges, the egg and pupal stages are unusually short, generally lasting only for a few days. Up to 10 months, however, is spent as a small maggot or caterpillar-like larva. And each species of midge has its own distinct or preferred habitat for its larva. While some species develop on the muddy margins of inland lochs, others exploit sea-coast marshes or farm-yards or drainage ditches. The Highland Midge larva grows from an egg on the blanket bogs, raised mires and poorly drained acidic grasslands that cover much of upland Britain, particularly in the wetter areas of the West. A suitable breeding site, for this species, is one which is relatively moist throughout the winter and summer but is reasonably free of standing water. Such sites are often marked by the presence of *Sphagnum* and *Polytrichum* mosses, particularly where there is some ground-water movement from the presence of nearby burns and ditches. To the botanist, the Jointed Rush *Juncus articulatus* is a good indicator of the larval breeding grounds of the Highland Midge. Just such sites are numerous throughout much of the West and Central Highlands. With some 4 million hectares at hand it is hardly surprising that enormous populations of midges can exist. Estimates of up to 24 million midge larvae per hectare (10 million per acre) have been made. It is likely that even these numbers are greatly exceeded in the coastal straths of the far West.

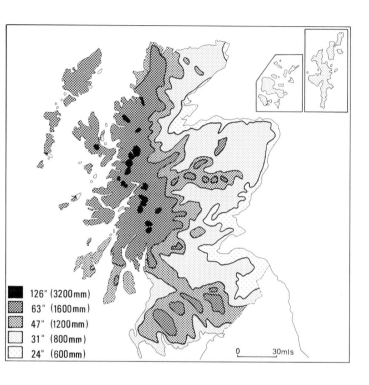

126" (3200 mm)
63" (1600 mm)
47" (1200 mm)
31" (800 mm)
24" (600 mm)

0   30mls

Average annual rainfall in Scotland. The Highland Midge
is found predominantly in areas where the rainfall exceeds
50" (1250 mm) a year.

In whatever habitat the eggs are laid, a critical aspect of midge survival is the need for moisture. Both the larvae and pupae are susceptible to desiccation. A dry spring and early summer can spell disaster for the new generation of midges but for humans and livestock it can signal a relatively midge-free season. A wet spring usually means a midgy summer. West of meridian 4°30′, within 60 km of the Atlantic seaboard, the average annual rainfall exceeds 1,250 mm (50 inches) and in some places regularly exceeds 2,500 mm (100 inches). These high-rainfall areas in the west of Scotland are the heart of the midge country. In the drier east, midges become less of a problem. Much of the east coast up to Aberdeenshire is comparatively free of midges though there are years when even the hardy Aberdonians suffer. Given the right habitat and sufficient rainfall, midges will breed by the millions.

The breeding cycle begins when the eggs are laid during the thirteen weeks of summer. In the case of the Highland Midge, the eggs are deposited two to five days after fertilisation in batches of fifty or more, probably on the surface of saturated humus or on wet vegetation close to the ground. After about ten to fourteen days the hatching larvae burrow into the top 5 cm of soil to develop, slowly, through five stages to mature, after Christmas, as a small, 5 mm-long, opaque-white caterpillar or maggot. While buried, the larvae acquire a voracious appetite and, during the ten months or so spent as a larva, the body length increases some six-fold. Capable of limited motion through moist soil, the omniverous

LIFE CYCLE AND DEVELOPMENTAL CALENDAR

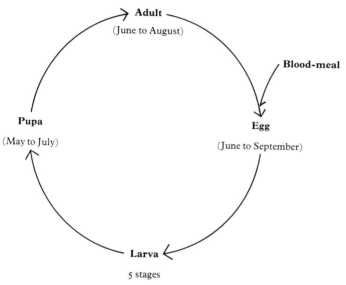

Adult
(June to August)

Blood-meal

Egg
(June to September)

Pupa
(May to July)

Larva
5 stages
(from August, over Autumn, Winter, Spring
to following summer)

midge larvae feed on a wide range of other larvae, threadworms, protozoa, green algae and, presumably, a wide selection of fungal spores and mycelia. Some species are not above a little cannibalism given the opportunity. When fully grown, from late April to July the larvae develop into the non-feeding pupal stage close to the surface of the soil. In some species, the pupae are capable of a flicking movement probably to counter the effects of desiccation. A prolonged drought at this critical stage may have a profound effect on the number of adults which finally emerge in the succeeding days. Good or bad midge-seasons, at least from a human viewpoint, will often depend on the rainfall in May and June as the pupae develop and mature. Prolonged dry weather has been shown to reduce populations of the Highland Midge by 90 per cent or more. Good, midge-free, days during summer can often be traced back to a dry spell in the preceding month.

The first adults to fly, at the end of May, seem to be predominantly male. Several midge species form gatherings of all-male swarms. They are rarely obvious, often short-lived and quite unlike the more familiar gatherings of the non-biting dancing midges. These male swarms, in the case of the biting midges, involve perhaps no more than a dozen or two individuals which hover and fly backwards and forwards, facing the wind, maintaining position over their chosen marker, often a puddle, an exposed rock or tree stump. Newly emerged females fly into the gathering to be promptly seized and mated. The fine

THIS IS THE LIFE, LADS -
WE GET FRUITFUL WHILE THE
LASSIES MULTIPLY

details of the mating process are not known, at least outside the laboratory, partly because of the inherent problem of trying to monitor the goings-on of a couple of busy insects only 2 mm long. The outcome, however, is at least predictable.

Either before or shortly after fertilisation, the females search for a source of carbohydrates and for a blood-meal. The carbohydrates, for energy, would ideally come from nectar but in the Highlands, in June and July, nectar-bearing flowers may not be widespread particularly over moorland. Other sources of energy are sought and may include sap-wounds from trees and rotting vegetation. But the critical step for the females is to secure a supply of fresh blood. For most midge species this is a key moment in reproduction; without it egg development is arrested and, given the short life-span of twenty, perhaps thirty, days for the adult, this is the point on which all future generations depend absolutely. So much is true for the greater majority of biting midge species in Scotland. However, the Highland Midge has one trick up its diminutive sleeve. Blood-meals are none too common in the Highlands. Ranging across the hills, glens and straths, humans and other large, warm-blooded mammals can be rare or even non-existent to an insect with a limited flight-range. The Highland Midge, unlike many other species, has partly solved this problem. It appears to have evolved a way of maturing and laying at least some of its first batch of eggs without a blood-meal. Whether it sacrifices part of its flight-muscle, which carries a similar nutrient to blood, in order to mature the eggs is not known for certain. This process of maturing even a few eggs in the absence of a blood-meal (known as autogeny) is perhaps central to the success of the Highland Midge. At least it ensures that there will be some survivors for next year. To develop further egg-batches however, a blood-meal is essential for this species. It is these females, having given birth once autogenously, which now form the bulk of the biting population. For good reason they are single-minded in their pursuit of blood.

Eventually, perhaps, a blood-meal is secured and at this point the females disappear (at least from all the collecting records). Although it is not known for certain, it seems most likely that these well-fed females seek cover and rest in long grass, heather or on nearby tree trunks where they quickly lose the urge for further biting. They no longer react to the evening stimulus to attack. Over the course of the next few days, the eggs steadily mature to be laid as before in a suitable damp breeding site. These eggs now represent the new generation which will emerge as flying adults the following year.

FLIGHT RANGE

In open country, over grassland and moorland, midges will drift passively for considerable distances particularly in uninterrupted light breezes. Under the right conditions in summer, large populations

FANCY HER GOING DRINKING
AND DANCING IN HER CONDITION.

can be carried 1,000 metres or more from the larval breeding grounds. Some hapless specimens have even been trapped many miles from land out in the North Sea. Others have been caught at considerable altitudes, from aircraft, in rising warm air-currents. The appearance of midges on some of the smaller West Coast islands unsuited to midge breeding such as Iona and Staffa, may be due to drifting from the neighbouring mainland. This long-distance passive movement of midges in light winds is one important reason why chemical larvicide spraying of the breeding grounds is ineffective, at least in Scotland. It makes no sense to attempt to treat the grounds surrounding, say, an isolated Highland hotel when a nearby population of hungry females will be blown in on the next favourable wind current.

In sheltered sites, particularly in established woodlands and in maturing forestry plantations, the adult midge population does not readily disperse far from the breeding grounds. Woodlands in the Highlands are often notoriously midgy sites partly because of the reduced light from shading trees and partly because the still air in forests does not promote passive drifting. Because of this the intensity of biting in a wood is usually directly related to the nearness of the actual breeding grounds.

Away from sheltered sites, midge intensity diminishes with elevation. Just as red deer seek relief from midges by moving to higher altitudes, so hill-walkers know that it is possible to avoid midge molestation on hillsides by climbing ever higher.

Indeed the relief to be gained from reaching an exposed windy site may be one good reason for driving the tired walker onwards to the summit.

THE IMPACT OF MIDGES ON THE HIGHLAND ECONOMY

The appearance of biting midges from late May to early September can be relied upon with confidence. Inevitably, this twelve to thirteen week period coincides with particular events in the Highland calendar. To the farmer and crofter in the West Highlands, this period is usually given over to the single hay crop and hay drying. This is also the period when much timber felling and extraction is carried out in the many forestry plantations. The summer months are the most productive period for road construction and repair. As autumn in the Highlands starts at the end of August and with snow falling as early as September or October, many trades and skills can only be effectively or reliably carried out during the midge season.

By far the greatest seasonal impact on the Highland economy is the welcome arrival of the summer visitors. They come from England, France, Germany, and in recent years from much further afield, with returning Scots from North America and Australasia, their arrival and departure being dictated mostly by national and school holidays. To adapt to this, many Highland hotels, guest houses, caravan- and camp-sites open for business only during the spring and summer. A number of restaurants, craft shops, museums and tourist information centres operate only in the summer weeks. A substantial element of the Highland economy thrives at precisely the period when midge biting is at its worst. Given that the three months of summer can play such a dominant part in the local economy, it is surprising to find that little has been published on the impact of midges on the Highland economy. Market research and consumer surveys have been conducted from time to time but their findings do not appear to have been made public. As a result there are a number of anecdotal and unsubstantiated stories about the impact of midges on Highland life. For example a leading firm of Glasgow Chartered Surveyors advises clients to avoid putting their houses on the market during the midge season; would-be purchasers quickly lose interest if pestered by midges. Deer and grouse shooters and game fishermen tend not to return next season if they have had to endure severe midgy days. Hotel keepers remark on the incidence of cancellations following a sequence of prolonged midgy evenings. And so on. But, away from the tourist trade, open reports are available on the impact of midges on other Highland industries. One report, for example, on the effect of biting midges on forestry showed that in the West Highlands, of the sixty-five working days of summer, up to 20 per cent of the time could be lost due to acute midge attacks on the forestry gangs. Of all occupations in the Highlands, forestry workers suffer badly from midge onslaughts. Hand-weeding and planting both involve working close to the ground vegetation and are notoriously prone to concentrated assaults. The work squads involved in timber felling have another kind of hell. There the men build up a fair sweat under their safety helmets and visors and create an odour that attracts midges in large numbers. As long as the chain saws are working the midges keep their distance, probably deterred by the exhaust fumes. But sooner or later the chain saws need refuelling or re-sharpening and this is the moment when the midges move in and drive grown men to near despair. Indeed there is an old saying among foresters that midges never attack a man standing with his hands in his pockets. But occupy his hands with a fencing maul, ditching spade or saw and the midges seem to know they can get a meal without being caught.

When the forestry workers return to their crofts in the evening, the midges are waiting for the intrepid soul who decides to cut or turn his hay. It is no laughing matter to see grown men raking the hay, with their heads and faces covered in their wives nylon stockings. Many other crofters are forced to stay inside on such evenings.

Forestry and, to some extent, crofting are part of the predictable future of the Highland economy. Both occupations have long ago adapted to the midge problem. What is less predictable is the return

LOOK, MORAG —
A FOOD
CHAIN

of the 13 to 14 million tourist trips made each year to Scotland. Such visitors spend almost £2 billion, a fair amount in midge country. And these valued visitors are often not aware of the midge problem until it bites them. There is then a strong case to be made for ensuring that these welcome guests come fully prepared for the midges. That way they may also be able to adapt quickly to the environment and enjoy their holidays to the full and to return in future years.

MIDGE CONTROL— IN FOLK MEDICINE

Man has had something like 8,000 years in which to learn to live with midges in Scotland. From the earliest times he may have been responsible, unwittingly, for the spread of the Highland Midge. There is strong evidence that substantial areas of the Highlands, now covered in blanket bog, were once comparatively well wooded and as a result well drained. The repeated findings of preserved tree stumps at the base of the bogs together with layers of charcoal indicates that Scotland's earliest inhabitants began the process of forest destruction by clear-felling and by fire. The landscape stripped of trees, now subject to erosion in the high rainfall areas, developed into the mire formations of *Sphagnum* bogs so familiar today. It is just such areas that form the core of the breeding grounds of the Highland Midge.

Alongside their first pastoral activities, the early settlers must have quickly learned how to cope with the midges. One simple but effective discovery would have been the smokey bonfire. The smoke from burning wood and peat appears to interfere in some way with the highly sensitive detectors on the midges' antennae and suppresses their ability to target potential victims. Smoke remains a useful deterrent to this day. The nearest equivalent to the portable smokey fire is the pipe full of tobacco, a device widely promoted for keeping midges at bay in several nineteenth century manuals on salmon fishing. The introduction of tobacco into Scotland in the early seventeenth century may have displeased King James VI but by then he was down in London and safely away from the midges. In succeeding years the efficacy of tobacco found a new meaning in Scotland. In the late nineteenth century English workmen were brought to the island of Rhum, there to build the castle for the Lancashire industrialist Sir George Bullough. Despite their Accrington origins, the poor souls were required to wear Sir George's Rhum tartan kilt. The midges must have been delighted by this obliging exposure of prime English leg. Poor Sir George nearly had a strike on his hands and only averted trouble by agreeing to pay his men a tobacco allowance of twopence a week. Although tobacco smoking is less favoured today, the resolution of ex-smokers has been cracked by midges in the past. Queen Victoria's water-colourist Carl

Haag was given the task of painting views of
Lochnagar, near Balmoral. Although this respected
and stalwart Austrian had publicly given up smoking
months earlier, it took just one really bad midgy
afternoon to compel him to send his servant back for
a box of cigars.

Herbal concoctions against midges have a long
history. The common plant Mugwort (*Artemisia
vulgaris*) owes its name to the old-English mycgwort,
literally midge-plant. A related species, Wormwood
(*Artemisia absinthium*) was recommended by Turner
in his sixteenth century herbal as an insect repellent
when used either as a lotion or when burnt on a fire.
Both of these species are related to tropical plants
which have long been exploited, commercially, for
their potent insecticidal properties. The active
ingredients are known as pyrethroids which in
nature presumably act to deter insects from feeding
on the plants. Some of these pyrethroids,
particularly the modern synthetic ones, are toxic not
just to insects but also to humans and should be
handled with care.

Over the centuries a number of plant extracts or
distillations to ward off insects have been described,
some of which are potent midge repellents. By the
1920s several anti-midge recipes had been published
using oils expressed or distilled from a wide range of
plants including Lavender, Lemon, Lemon-grass,
Fleabane, Wormwood, Geranium, Bitter Orange,
White Cedar, Cypress, Eucalyptus, Dill, Fennel,
Juniper, Tansy and Thyme. Despite this long list, all
of these plants contain a small number of

chemically-related oils called terpenoids. Certain of these terpenoids such as limonene, pinene, thujone and citronella are proven and powerful insecticides. All have a strong and characteristic aroma and indeed several have been used in perfumes, shampoos and soaps. Pinene, for example, has been used in household floor-cleaners to impart a smell of country freshness, citronella is widely employed to give a lemon-smell to shampoos. Whether or not washing with such shampoos has any effect on midges has not been recorded. Thujone, found in Red and White Cedars (*Thuja* spp.), does seem to have an effect on midges; the old foresters in the days before chemical repellents used to deliberately have their lunch by a *Thuja* hedge or tree to keep the midges at bay. But it was citronella which was most widely used as a pre-war midge repellent. The Forestry Commission used to issue gallon-jars of citronella to their workforce, right up to the 1950s. This had the reputation of turning the user an olive-yellow colour with continuous application. It has its adherents to this day and it can still be found for sale, occasionally, in a few Highland pharmacies.

Following the recent revival of interest in herbal alternatives to man-made chemical repellents, some of the old remedies are once again being offered for sale. One enterprising Australian company is marketing a blend of natural repellents which includes oil of citronella, pennyroyal, cajuput, lavender, bergamot and sassafras. The end product has a pleasant smell and in a brief trial against the midges of Gairloch it was declared satisfactory.

Interestingly, one of the components, sassafras, comes from a tree which used to be prescribed to ward off the effects of the ague (or malaria).

In Australia where the coastal midges can be a serious nuisance, the Queensland sea-anglers have developed their own insect repellent. Having drunk the contents of a beer bottle or can, they half fill it with vegetable oil, add a quarter of a cupful of an antisepetic liquid such as Dettol, top up with water and shake vigorously. The foaming emulsion is then applied liberally to all exposed parts. Visiting midges may be deterred by the smell of carbolic acid or if not they will drown in the vegetable oil, it is claimed. The recipe has the advantage over most commercial repellents that it does not contaminate the bait nor dissolve nylon tackle.

A more recent and probably unplanned discovery was made in the Florida Everglades. There, both midges and other biting flies are a serious menace to visitors. However some adventurous souls dicovered that by swathing themselves in a bath-lotion marketed as Avon Skin-So-Soft, they were able to keep the midge bites to a tolerable level. It may well be that small insects simply drown in the sticky lotion, though it is true that the ingredients include at least one compound which might well ward off insects (as well as promoting soft skin).

In the scientific literature, there are regular reports of plants which are discovered to have potent anti-mosquito (and presumably anti-midge) proper-ties. Most of these plants come from the tropics and warmer climates though many have relatives among our native flora or among our common garden plants. *Delphinium staphisagria* from the Mediterranean region is one. *Spilanthes mauritiana* from Kenya, a relative of *Helianthus* and *Dahlia* spp. contains a powerful mosquito larvicide. It would be an interesting and useful challenge to cultivate a midge-free garden in the Highlands by trying to grow some of these species here. For those gardeners willing to try, two groups of plant worth considering for their anti-midge potential are those in the tribes Heliantheae and Anthemidae of the Compositae. With over 5,000 species in these groups there should be plenty to choose from. A midge-free garden in the Highlands would certainly make the headlines.

But perhaps a more simple way of coping with midges lies in another characteristic common to midges and indeed mosquitoes. These insects are attracted to dark colours. Scientists have long used black cloths laid over the ground specifically to catch midges alive, for further study. One explanation for this preference for dark colours is that many midge species take their rest on dark-coloured vegetation including tree-trunks. This ties in with the crofters' claim that the old breed of sandy-coloured Highland Cattle suffered less from the midges than did the Black Cattle. This is not an observation confined to Scotland. Experienced entomologists working in Africa often trap mosquitoes and midges using black cloths. In Russia, midges have been recorded searching for and landing on stationary dark-coloured cars, while avoiding light-coloured vehicles. Although proper trials seem not to have been conducted, this repeatedly observed preference for dark colours should not be ignored. It would make sense to wear light-coloured clothing whenever midges are about.

CONTROL—THROUGH CHEMICAL REPELLENTS

It was with considerable foresight that the Secretary of State for Scotland, Tom Johnston, in 1944 asked his scientific advisors to find out if there was a suitable chemical repellent available which could be used against midges. Johnston was no doubt aware of the war-time campaigns fought against mosquitoes to control malaria and other diseases in the battle-grounds of south-east Asia. There, the allied forces were using various newly-released insect repellents, including one developed at the then Royal Technical College in Glasgow called dimethyl phthalate. DMP or Dimp, from ex-Army stocks, became the subject of intensive study in the Scottish Highlands. Quite what Johnston's motives were in promoting this research is not recorded. However, as an active founder and chairman of the then North of Scotland Hydro-Electric Board, he had first-hand experience of Scottish midges in the remote areas of the North-West. It was also rumoured that several army camps and naval bases in the West Highlands had become, at times, almost untenable in the midgy summers of 1943 and 1944. A mid-August walk today out to the old gun-emplacements near Aultbea will give some idea of the misery of sentry duty in those war years. The sites abound with midges which seem to choose the now abandoned buildings to shelter from the wind.

Johnston's scientific advisors, drawn from each of the Scottish universities, set to work in the summer of 1945. One team undertook a large-scale survey, throughout Scotland, to determine the number of different species present and which ones were doing most of the biting. Of the fifteen species then known (today thirty-four are recognised) the team identified one species, *C. impunctatus*, the Highland Midge, as responsible for 90 per cent or more of the trouble. This was enough information to set the second group into action. Based on headquarters at Raigmore Hospital in Inverness, field trials of the DMP repellent were set up initially at Achnashellach, Ross-shire, and at Auchterawe, near Fort Augustus, places deep in the heart of the midge country. With the co-operation of volunteers from the Forestry Commission and with help from Land Army girls, roadmen, crofters, fishermen and school-teachers from Skye to Sutherland, a methodical testing of DMP began. Within two seasons a satisfactory formulation had been developed and tested under West Coast weather conditions. Applied as a liquid or as a gel directly to the skin, or used to impregnate veils and clothing,

DMP rapidly gained approval. Its effectiveness, compared to the older pre-war repellents such as citronella, was quickly established and a Scottish manufacturer was found. From the late 1940s, DMP became available to the general public. Within a few years a second repellent appeared on the market, again from anti-mosquito campaigns, called di-ethyl toluamide or DEET. These two compounds DMP and DEET form the basis for most of the midge repellents sold in Britain today and indeed overseas. The repellents come in several forms. The most concentrated form is as a liquid, currently available at concentrations of 70 to 80 per cent (45 per cent in the case of DMP). Higher concentrations become noticeably oily. Surveys among British and US forces found that Deet at 75 per cent concentration was sufficient to repel mosquitoes, higher concentrations offering no real advantage. Rather more expensive are the same ingredients packaged as aerosols, often complete with ozone-destroying propellants. The concentration of repellent in the cans varies among the competing brands from around 12 per cent to 55 per cent, the difference being reflected in the price. As the propellant in these aerosols evaporates, what is left behind on the skin is 100 per cent repellent. In terms of value for money, most of the liquid preparations are a better buy than the aerosols. At lower concentrations, DEET is marketed in the form of gels and creams with the repellent concentration reduced to between 5 per cent and 35 per cent. For the seriously troubled, liquid preparations are probably the most cost-effective. Several of the repellent manufacturers claim that their liquid products offer up to eight hours protection. In fairness this assertion may be valid for the more sedentary user in cool temperatures but for those undertaking any exercise resulting in increased perspiration, the liquid can lose its effectiveness in one or two hours.

Although only the two compounds DMP and DEET are widely marketed as midge repellents, they come in many different brand names and prices. The most common ones are Autan, Boots Insect Repellent, Jungle Formula, Mijex and Secto-Combat (all containing DEET) or Shoo (DMP-based). Other brands imported from North America and occasionally sold by mail-order include another batch of DEET-based compounds such as Deepwoods Off !, Repel, Cutter, Muskol and Space Shield. Some products may contain a little glycerol to counteract any drying of the skin. Apart from attractive packaging and presentation, the difference between the competing brands rests on price. Purchasers are urged to look at the price in relation to concentration. The price charge by one company, a household name, currently does not stand well against some of the smaller companies. Other so-called insect repellents are marketed from time to time, often with cosmetic or restorative attributes implied by the names 'milk', 'cream' or 'balm'. Usually based on ethyl hexanediol (or a similar sounding synonym), their effectiveness against midges is questionable.

Accepting that the most widely used midge

repellents contain either DEET or DMP, how safe and how effective are they? On safety, both repellents have been used in the plastics industry to soften hard plastics. The repellent manufacturers sensibly warn their customers to avoid bringing their products into contact with plastics, spectacle frames, polished or painted surfaces, rayon or acetate. Both DMP and DEET have been marketed as midge and mosquito repellents for over forty years, throughout the tropics, in Australia and North America. Apart from the relatively small number of adults with unusually sensitive skins, there is no solid evidence to indicate that these compounds are not safe when correctly and sensibly used. Incorrectly used they are toxic and if drunk can lead to acute poisoning. It has also long been known that many repellents are capable of being absorbed by the skin. It makes sense then to treat *all* repellents with caution. The British medical journal 'The Lancet' recently published the following advice on the use of DEET (the journal has yet to consider the use of the other commonly available repellents based on DMP). The advice is as follows:

> When used sensibly insect repellents are advantageous and safe, but the potential toxicity of DEET is high and the use of repellents containing more than 50% DEET should be avoided in infants and young children because of their thinner skin. Frequent total body application of DEET for days or weeks should be avoided.

These are sensible precautions which are followed by

most users. If these repellents were suspected as being unsafe in normal use, the various medicine and drug-regulating bodies throughout the world, and particularly in the United States, would long ago have called their safety into question. Instead these repellents are the standard authorised issue to the armed forces of the United States, Canada and India. The international acceptance of DMP and DEET-based repellents for so many years is a fair indicator of their safeness. It is not, however, an indicator that they are the best.

Active research into devising new and safe repellents goes on in several overseas countries, usually coupled to particular types of biting flies. None have been approved for unregulated use by the public at large, at least not in those countries which control the sale and use of medicines. It does seem probable however, that more effective repellents will be approved in the next few years and one or more may be found to be particularly effective against the Highland Midge. Certain of these compounds are currently under field-test overseas, some against tropical species of midges. However, for the moment, the best that is available in Scotland are the DEET or DMP-based products.

There is, however, scope for improving the effectiveness of the currently-available repellents. In 1946, when DMP was undergoing field trials in the Highlands, volunteers were asked to wear net veils previously impregnated with the repellent. The responses were highly favourable but for various reasons, including perhaps the design or weight of the cloth, use of the veils was discontinued. More recently veils, or more correctly net jackets with hoods, have been manufactured and sold in the United States aimed at the hunter and game-fisher. These loosely woven, light-weight, jackets come complete with press studs and draw strings. They need to be impregnated from time to time, perhaps once every few days, by simply shaking the jacket in a specially designed bag containing the DEET-based repellent. Limited trials of the jacket have been conducted in Scotland, by coincidence near Achnashellach, Ross-shire, the location of the original post-war midge repellent trials. One discerning Achnashellach resident, well known for his seven-acre garden, found that the midge jacket allowed him to work in the most midgy sites well into the evening. Without the jacket, some of his tasks had to be left over to the sunniest days when midge activity was low. A local crofter was able to turn his hay in the evenings, a task considered to be almost impossible after eight o'clock without the impregnated jacket. When freshly impregnated, the jacket is highly effective against the Highland Midge, it is comfortable to wear and does not appear to impede movement. Its drawback is that it is relatively expensive and could only really be recommended for those who are likely to be exposed to severe midge attacks throughout the season. The simple message would seem to be that, until something better comes along, DMP or DEET-based products, particularly those sold as liquids, are the most effective currently available.

CONTROL—BY INSECTICIDES AND LARVICIDES

After the launching of the first of the midge repellents in Scotland in 1946, a scientific push was made towards tackling the major problem; how to eliminate midges and midge breeding from areas close to human settlements? At that time almost nothing was known about the ten-month long larval stages of the midge, so the first attempts to eradicate the insect were made against the flying adult. It was already established from work carried out in the United States and in the Pacific that mosquitoes could be controlled over large areas by spraying insecticides from aircraft. However, attempts to deal with midges in a similar way had proved much less successful, at least in the Far East. In addition, the economics of employing aircraft and specialised spraying equipment for no more than two months of the year in remote areas of the Highlands compelled the scientists to look at alternative ways of tackling the adult flying midge. Barrier spraying had been developed during the war to protect military camps from the nightly assaults of malarial mosquitoes. Strips of land 50 yards wide, regularly doused with DDT, had proved successful at keeping several mosquito species at bay. The decision was made to try out barrier sprays at selected sites in Scotland.

Several acres of moorland and woodland were treated with insecticides at concentrations known to kill most insects. The outcome was entirely unexpected. To all intents the adult midges appeared to be quite unaffected. As soon as the spraying operations were completed the midges emerged to resume their activities. It was not the DDT that was at fault. In laboratory tests midges, like most other insects, were readily knocked down by this highly toxic insecticide. From investigations in the field it appeared that midges were able to avoid all contact with the insecticide spray, probably by hiding instinctively on the underside of the vegetation. This ties in with the observation that midges at rest seek out dark colours and shaded sites. Barrier spraying was then spectacularly unsuccessful. Similar results were subsequently obtained overseas during midge control programmes. From this it was clear that the diminutive midge had one up on its big cousin the mosquito.

If nothing could be done against the adult then the next target was the larva. Apart from knowing little about the larva itself, next to nothing was known about the larval breeding sites. This gap in basic knowledge was a serious drawback. It was reasoned that if the breeding areas could be located on the ground then larvicides could be targeted to just those areas supporting breeding colonies. Identifying the precise location had another benefit; the toxic sprays could be restricted to areas away from livestock. Under Dr Douglas Kettle (later to become a world authority on midges) a team from the University of Glasgow set out to locate the breeding grounds. Using specially designed traps which caught the newly emerged adult it proved possible to identify with considerable precision the breeding preferences of many of the Scottish species. Some species chose muddy farmyards, others preferred shaded woodland pools, freshwater ponds or stagnant mires. The Highland Midge, however, was found in none of these. Instead it was restricted to the damper areas of rough grazing and moorland, characteristically bearing *Sphagnum* and *Polytrichum* mosses and the jointed rush, *Juncus articulatus*. These plants now became the tell-tale for the otherwise hidden larval breeding sites. Closer examination revealed the small elusive maggots buried within the top inch of soil. These were the sites where the adult midges laid their eggs in the previous summer and which now bore next year's generation of adults in the form of larvae.

With the continued support of the Scottish Department of Health and with help from the Carnegie Trust and the Scottish Tourist Board, battle lines were set up in the form of a Midge Control Unit, under Dr Kettle, now based at the University of Edinburgh. Throughout the 1950s, a series of field trials were conducted on the hills outside Edinburgh and also at Talladale by Loch Maree in Ross-shire. tests with several potent larvicides showed that the degree of effectiveness at killing the larvae depended on sufficient rain-fall to wash the chemicals into the soil. Without rain the insecticides were largely ineffective. The second observation was that once washed into the soil, the toxins were highly effective in reducing midge numbers. Rather more profound was the discovery that the larvicides persisted in the soil for several years. Unfortunately these persistent insecticides, widely used 30 years ago, had toxic effects on much more than just midges. The introduction of a chemical toxin into a food chain inevitably means that animals higher up the chain, including birds and mammals, will accumulate the insecticide from their diet. Because all animals, from insects to Man, obey the same biological principles, what is toxic to an insect is frequently potentially toxic to all higher forms of life if the dose is raised in proportion to the body-weight of the animal. The result of Man's profligate use of these insecticides and other toxic chemicals was graphically recounted by Rachel Carson in her best-selling book *Silent Spring*. As governments throughout the world began to recognise the devastating effects on wildlife by the late 1960s, attempts to control midge breeding by the use of broad-spectrum chemical sprays was largely ended, both in Scotland and overseas. In recent years rather more sophisticated chemical insecticides have become available which are either short-lived or claim to have a degree of specificity against one or a few groups of insects. These insecticides allegedly have much less harmful effects on the environment. Several are used in seasonal combat against mosquitoes. In the United States, and elsewhere, local self-help organisations have been formed to control mosquitoes usually by methodically treating swamps and lakes by ground-based chemical fogging, or mist spraying, or by spraying larger areas from the air. No serious attempts have been undertaken in Scotland against the midge and the reason is simple enough. During the larvicide trials in Scotland in the 1950s, there was one quite unexpected finding which once again showed that the midge has one up on the mosquito. When an area had been thoroughly doused in the appropriate larvicide and the rain had washed the toxin into the soil the midge larvae were of course killed. However within days midge attacks were resumed. It appeared that adult midges from areas perhaps up to one mile away were moving in to bite in the sprayed zones. The only way to have eliminated these intruders would have been to extend the larvicide treatment several miles into the hills, an impossibly expensive operation. The monetary cost of such an operation confined to even the most severely affected areas would have been prohibitive. The ecological cost to Scotland's wildlife would have been unthinkable. For these reasons the use of larvicides against the Highland Midge, whether on a small community scale or over a larger land-mass, does not seem to be a practical solution to the midge problem.

CONTROL—THROUGH HABITAT MANIPULATION

The problem of how to tackle the midge is not confined to Scotland. Many attempts have been made overseas, sometimes with unfortunate consequences, but occasionally with considerable success. For example in Australia the midge breeding grounds have been tackled fairly effectively by altering the physical environment of the site. In parts of Queensland some relief has been secured by clear-felling and back-filling the mangrove swamps, or altering the steepness of the shore-line and canal-side breeding sites. By damming or draining tidal inlets, it has proved possible to destroy midge larval habitats on a long-tem basis. However, even these often costly landscaping efforts have occasionally back-fired. At one Caribbean paradise development, cursed by biting midges, the local hoteliers helped to finance the drainage of a nearby mangrove swamp, known to support a thriving colony of larvae. Having spent much money landscaping the reclaimed area, the developers were not pleased to find a new species of midge on the wing; one which was a more vicious biter and particularly active during the evening cocktail hour. The second species had previously been unable to establish itself in the area because of the wet conditions of the mangrove. But as soon as the site had been drained, the vicious biter found its own breeding paradise. Other developers have learnt from this experience and more successful landscaping has involved damming rather than draining the lagoons, so keeping a permanent stand of water between the midge and its chance to lay eggs. In Scotland, it is doubtful if any attempt to alter the landscape of localised areas would be successful in the long-term. There the Highland Midge appears to be more mobile than its Caribbean cousins and seems capable of drifting from distant breeding grounds right into the centre of towns and villages. Built-up areas in the Highlands such as Oban, Portree or Stornoway can be several hundred yards from the nearest extensive breeding grounds; yet, given the right wind conditions, midges can on occasions move into the centre of these small towns and make life uncomfortable. Only the most extensive programme of land drainage or water impoundment is likely to have any worthwhile effect.

Reviewing the past forty years of research into Scottish midges, the initial support for chemical spraying of adult midges or their larvae has now been lost because the field trials proved to be ineffective or had unacceptable consequences for wild life. Despite these set-backs the research and field trials have provided much useful information about the way midges live. One benefit has been the development of repellents which, for all their faults, have offered considerable relief to the resident and visiting population. Knowing how to spot a probable midge breeding ground has enabled architects and builders to choose sites at least to windward of midgy grounds. Now that we understand something about the life cycle and biting habits of midges, locals and visitors with a little experience can now predict the likelihood of good or bad midgy days.

CONTROL—FUTURE PROSPECTS

Left alone, the midges will continue to cause misery to visitors and locals alike. They will continue to disrupt man's activities in forest plantations, in shepherding, stock-rearing and hay-making. They will displease hotel-keepers and their guests, annoy game fishers and deer shooters and irritate hill-walkers, hitch-hikers and campers. On occasions the midges will drive these good folk away with vows of never returning to the Highlands again. This is adverse publicity for the Highlands and it is therefore all the more strange that the various organisations concerned with tourism should keep silent about the problem. Silence will not lessen the problem and lays the promoters of tourism open to charges of being less than truthful. There is an alternative approach based partly on open discussion about midges and partly by tackling the problem by using the latest scientific developments in insect control. Although biting midges will never be eradicated from Scotland short of a major climatic upheaval, there are ways of reducing the midge problem to levels which are both bearable and which will allow the full benefits of the Highlands to be enjoyed throughout the summer.

Research into midge control virtually ceased in Scotland in the mid-1960s. Overseas, research has continued, particularly in the United States, East Africa and in Australia, stimulated from time to time by outbreaks of midge-borne diseases in horses and sheep and irate local authorities and tourist boards. In addition the governments of several developed and third-world countries support research into insect control for good military reasons. Midges along with mosquitoes and blackflies can severely impede the ability of ground troops to live off the countryside, whether in northern Canada or in southern India. All this has helped to fund research into new methods of control of the local species of midge. Scotland's midge problem, though acute by any standard, does not attract its share of research and development resources. Its small indigenous repellent industry together with that based in England has not produced any fundamentally new products for over thirty years. The prospects may be that nothing new will happen until someone tries out a product developed abroad against say Venezuelan midges or the sand flies of Tasmania. Such a trial would be a gamble for an entrepreneur; the scientific literature is full of examples of repellents which have proved to be highly effective against one midge species but quite ineffective against another. The last repellent trials recorded in Scotland, conducted specifically against the Highland Midge, were carried out in 1947. The Forestry Commission has from time to time re-appraised new offerings from the repellent industry but always based on DMP or DEET.

There are three areas in which coordinated research is required if the purely Scottish midge problem is going to be solved. The first is to assess just what is the impact of biting midges on the Scottish, and particularly the Highland, economy. Conducted by trained assessors, such an investigation would establish the cost to the forestry, farming and crofting, electricity, transport and communications industries of work disrupted and lost as a result of midge attacks. The investigation would assess the cost to that key element of the Highland economy, tourism. Given this information, it might then be possible to direct efforts into particular sectors of the economy as well as identifying which industry or trade would support, financially, further research.

The second area of effort, long overdue, would be to look at the repellents that have been developed overseas and to see if they are effective against the Highland Midge. Trials conducted under strictly defined, scientifically approved, criteria would be carried out in the field under the varied climatic conditions of the Scottish Highlands. A number of tests have evolved over the years where groups of volunteers, male and female, young and old, are asked to apply a sequence of repellents usually to one arm only and then to subject themselves to foraging midges. Ideally the volunteers should be closely monitored while carrying out various tasks related to their normal occupations. To eliminate the likelihood that midges might be attracted to one individual more than another, each volunteer takes turn to test each repellent. Such trials, conducted by trained technicians under medical and scientific control, have frequently shown that one particular repellent works well under one set of weather conditions or is effective against one species of midge but is less effective under other conditions or against other species. So far as is known, rigourously controlled, modern-day, trials against the Highland Midge have never been conducted, neither in Scotland nor in Western Europe. The goal of such trials would be to identify which of the modern range of repellents are superior to DMP or DEET against the Highland Midge on its home ground. With sound medical and scientific backing, manufacturers or importers would be given the confidence to invest in new, safer and more effective ways of tackling the midge problem. While the immediate benefit would pass quickly to the consumer, the longer-term gain would fall to those concerned with the Highland economy, including rural industry and tourism. Having provided an opportunity to assess the social and economic costs of the biting midge and having secured at least a short-term solution through modern repellents, the third and most fundamental area of research would remain.

Just as the military commander remembers the

maxim to know your enemy, so there remains much that is unknown about the ways of the Highland Midge. If radically new ways are to be sought for tackling the midge problem, then a new understanding of the midge is badly needed, particularly in the fields of insect physiology and behaviour. Some of this information would be easy to secure. For example, it is already possible to predict 'good' and 'bad' midgey days, at least on a local level. It would take no great stretch of the imagination to visualise a 'midge forecast' on local or regional radio or in the newspapers in much the same way as pollen forecasts are made for the benefit of hay-fever sufferers down south. Forewarned, people might then be able to plan their day so as to avoid the worst of the assaults. To put this forecasting on to a solid and reliable basis some fundamental field studies would have to be resumed from the point where they were left off in the late 1960s. Almost nothing is known of the effect of climate on the process of selecting breeding grounds and egg-laying. This is a critical point in the life cycle. After egg laying, does the midge immediately set out for a new blood meal or is there a delay? Where does the fully gorged midge go to while her eggs mature? What attracts the female Highland Midge to the male swarms? And, indeed, what is the odour that attracts the midge to its victim, often over considerable distances? And what part does the weather play in all this? These and many other questions need to be answered before scientists can predict midge behaviour tomorrow and next week.

There is one area of research which perhaps has more promise than any other of solving the midge problem. This is what is called 'biological control'. At its simplest this means the control (or even the elimination) of one undesirable organism by another, less undesirable, biological component. The biological component may be a predator introduced into an area because it specifically seeks out and kills the unwanted species. An example is the deliberate introduction of a cat on to a rat-infested island. Today, the biological component is often a disease, viral or bacterial which is intentionally spread to bring about the demise of a pest species. An example is the deliberate spread of a particular virus which destroys the Pine Beauty Moth larva, a menace capable of devastating the forest plantations of Scotland. Other insect pests are being tackled, overseas, by the introduction of genetically engineered bacteria which are pathogenic to the pest in question and, seemingly, to no other. One such organism *Bacillus thuringensis*, once it has been suitably 'modified', is used in tests against certain midge species. Whether or not this pathogen would be effective against the Highland Midge has yet to be investigated. It is also possible to transfer anti-midge genes cut from *B. thuringensis* into plants. There the genes express themselves and promptly cause the death of insects which choose to feed upon the transformed plants. What prevents this powerful weapon being used against Scottish midges is that we have no clear idea what plants are fed upon by the male and female midges. This relatively unsophisticated but essential research has never been done.

Midges undoubtedly have their natural enemies, animal, fungal or bacterial, and it may be possible to use these to control the midge population. For example the midges round the Tay and the Forth on the East Coast are sometimes infected by a minute parasitic worm. These Mermithid parasites appear to specialise in living inside the midge larvae without actually killing their host. Instead the poor old midge, when it becomes an adult, develops a mix of male and female sex organs and is effectively sterile. If these parasites were to be introduced on a wide scale into the major breeding grounds of the Highland Midge, they could make a significant impact on the insect population. There is only one problem: little work has been done on the parasite in Scotland for twenty years. Questions like how to breed up the worm and how and when it invades the midge larvae are not known. Nor have the consequences for wildlife at large been worked out. There is then a need for well-directed research to be conducted employing the latest thinking on biological control as a way of dealing with the midge problem.

The inevitable question that arises when science offers a possible solution is who pays for the research before the development? And the inevitable answer is the customer. The customers, those who stand to benefit from the research, include the local Highland communities, the summer visitors whether as transient coach parties or longer-stay hotel guest, sportsmen including game-fishermen on the Spey and climbers on the Munroes. Others to benefit will include those who earn at least part of their living from the tourist trade whether as keepers of hotels, youth hostels, craft shops or from one of the many other businesses which thrive during the summer season. The Highland industries represented by forestry, fishing, fishfarming, crofting, weaving and knitting would also benefit to some degree from midge control. In addition, other groups are concerned about biting midges but may live out of the region. These will include the medical and veterinary professions charged with health care in Scotland and the chemical and pharmaceutical industry involved in the manufacture, import and distribution of midge repellents, insecticides and related products. With such diffuse interests it is unlikely that any single group would be willing to finance all of the research needed to alleviate the midge problem. There is then a need for a central body to initiate and to promote research. Forty years ago the initiative was taken by the Secretary of State for Scotland with funding principally from the Department of Health and the Scottish Tourist Board. If the will is there to support the research, then new answers will be found to tackle the midge problem. But it does need a lead.

THE ECOLOGICAL SIGNIFICANCE OF MIDGES

Whatever Man has tried to do to control the activities of midges, there remains the hard fact that midges in turn have been controlling Man's activities for many many years. Whether or not this age-old struggle will continue in the midges' favour remains to be seen. But quite apart from their relationship with humans, the biting midges have an important and enduring relationship with many of the other creatures that go to make up the natural history of the Highlands.

At one level, midges like most other insects, are part of a complex food web. The sheer number of midges, and particularly midge larvae, throughout the West Highlands are bound to make an impact on the lives of other organisms whether as prey or as a food-source. The exact role played by midge larvae in these food chains can only be guessed at, for this is another neglected area of scientific research. It is known, however, that the midge larvae are the food source for several types of soil-dwelling inverte-brates, including nematode worms. Similarly, the omniverous midge larvae prey heavily on other soil organisms as can be seen from their five- or six-fold increase in body length in nine or ten months. Because they are a component of one or more food chains, then any episode, natural or man-made, which significantly alters the size of the midge larval population will inevitably have a knock-on effect on the other inhabitants of the soil. Droughts in early summer, for example, are known to drastically reduce midge numbers, though unfortunately it is not known what effect this has on other creatures. In a similar way, persistent larvicides and other toxins will have effects not just on midge larvae but on all those creatures which directly or indirectly rely on midges as a food source.

Leaving aside the poorly understood world of the larvae, it is the impact made by the flying adult midge which has attracted Man's attention and more often his wrath. This impact lies at the heart of the ecology of the Highlands because it directly modifies Man's activities. Midges are abundant in the high rainfall areas of the Highlands in precisely the places which have long proved to be the most difficult to cultivate and maintain. Here both Man and his domestic animals have struggled to secure some sort of productive and ordered life for the past 4,000 years or so. Until recently this struggle was confined largely to the coastal strips, straths and glens. The broader expanses of moorland, woodland and high hills have long been considered to be, at best, half tamed. The principal reason for this is that the environment allows just a degree of exploitation before it responds by becoming even more harsh. The stripping of the wild forests from the lower hillsides in the past millenium has left behind land which has fallen to the ever-encroaching blanket bog and ill-drained moorland. Into this impoverished landscape the Highland Midge has moved to become, today, a dominant member of the natural wildlife, far more significant than golden eagles, pine martens or the wild cat. Having achieved this dominance over the Highlands, the biting midge should be recognised as an important element in limiting Man's activities. Within the context of Western Europe, the Scottish Highlands are one of the most under-populated landscapes with a timelessness difficult to find anywhere in the late twentieth century. This is the area where Man has a foothold and no more. If, as seems likely, the biting midge is a significant factor in limiting our activities then this diminutive guardian of the Highlands deserves our respect.

APPENDIX

BITING MIDGE (*CULICOIDES*) SPECIES FROM SCOTLAND

Species	Frequency	Larval breeding sites			Comments
C. achrayi	Uncommon	Loch margins	(+)	Horses	Biting habit lost?
C. albicans	Common	Wetter bog areas	o	o	Early season flier
C. brunnicans	Uncommon	Streamsides	(+)	—	Argyll only?
C. cameroni	Rare	Waterfall habitat	—	—	Diminutive size
C. chiopteris	Common	Cow dung	(+)	Cattle, horses	
C. circumscriptus	Locally common	Coastal salt marshes	—	—	
C. clintoni	Rare	Shady boggy sites	—	—	
C. delta	Common	Wet areas, moor	(+)	Cattle, horses	Early season flier
C. dewulfi	Common	Cow dung	—	Horses	Cause of sweet itch of horse?
C. duddingstoni	Locally common	Loch margins	—	—	
C. fascipennis	Common	Wetland mud	(+)	—	
C. griscens	Common	Marshes	(+)	—	
C. halophilus	Locally common	Coastal brackish pools	+	—	Overwinters as eggs
C. heliophilus	Frequent	Sphagnum bogs	+++	Dogs, sheep	Painful biter
C. impunctatus	Abundant	Sphagnum bogs	+++	Cattle, deer, poultry	Daytime flier
C. kibunensis	Frequent	Marshes, loch margins	—	Horses, birds	
C. lupicaris	Uncommon	Exposed mud	(+)	Cattle, horses	

Species	Abundance	Habitat	Biting habit	Hosts	Biting habit lost?
C. manchuriensis	Uncommon	Coastal salt marshes	o	o	
C. maritimus	Locally common	Coastal salt marshes	—	—	
C. nubeculosus	Locally common	Farmyards (dung)	+++	Horses, birds	Vector of fistulous withers
C. obsoletus	Abundant	Decaying plants, wetland	+++	Cattle, sheep, goats	Principally in Lowlands
C. odibilis	Frequent	Exposed mud	—	Poultry	
C. pallidicornis	Frequent	Marshy ground	(+)	Horses, birds	Early season flier
C. pictipennis	Common	Woodland pools	(+)	Birds	
C. poperinghensis	Rare	Tay salt marshes	—	—	Flies May to October
C. pulicaris	Locally common	Muddy marshes	+	Horses, cattle, sheep	Causes sweet itch of horse?
C. punctatus	Frequent	Muddy marshes	+	Horses, cattle, sheep	
C. reconditus	Uncommon	Not known	—	—	Daytime flier
C. riethi	Locally common	Forth, Tay salt marshes	—	Horses	Strathclyde Region
C. riouxi	Rare	Not known	—	—	Common on Beauly Firth
C. salinarius	Uncommon	Coastal salt flats	—	—	
C. scoticus	Rare	On fungi?, wetland	—	—	
C. segnis	Uncommon	Not known	—	—	April to June flier
C. stigma	Common	Exposed mud	+	Horses	Day flier, April-May

Key: Biting habit: + + + = persistent biter of Man; + = less frequently attacks Man; (+) = occasionally bites Man; — = biting habit not known; o = biting habit probably lost.

BIBLIOGRAPHY

There are few readily obtainable (and readable) books on biting midges, but for those who would like to delve into the scientific literature, a brief list is given below. It is generally possible to borrow the appropriate journal through the public libraries. The selection given can only be the tip of the iceberg but at least it is the more readable tip.

1. Books with broad-based accounts of biting midges together with related insects and their impact throughout the world:

    Kettle, D S (1984) *Medical and Veterinary Entomology*. Croom Helm, London

    Service, M W (1986) *Bloodsucking Insects: vectors of disease*. Studies in Biology Series No. 167. Edward Arnold,London.

2. Scientific accounts from which the reader can delve further:

    Boorman, J (1986) British Culicoides (Diptera: Ceratopogonidae). Notes on distribution and biology. *Entomology Gazette 37* pp 253–66.

Campbell, J A and Pelham-Clinton, E C (1960) A taxonomic review of the British species of Culicoides. *Proceedings of the Royal Society of Edinburgh. B* 67 pp181-302.

Edwards, F W, Oldroyd, H and Smart, J (1939) *British Blood-sucking Flies* British Museum. London.

Hendry, G A F and Godwin, G (1988) Biting Midges in Scottish forestry. *Scottish Forestry 42* pp. 113-19.

Kettle, D S (1969) Ecology and Control of Blood-sucking Ceratopogonids. *Acta Tropica 26* pp 235-248.

Kettle, D S (1961) A study on the association between moorland vegetation and the breeding sites of Culicoides. *Bulletin of Entomological Research 52* pp 381-411.